The Widow Who Saved Her Town

By

Angie Braucher

Published by: Midnight Publishing
Vero Beach, Fl

ISBN: 9798334748866

The Widow Who Saved Her Town

Chapter 1

In the small town of Leewood, South Carolina, lived a widow named Jane Knox. Leewood was the kind of town where everyone knew everyone. Most of the men in town worked at ShoeWorks, a factory that produced a variety of shoes wholesale around the world.

Jane was a short woman with a small frame. She had been a widow for 7 years now. She was struggling financially. She was only receiving a small pension check from the factory. Her husband worked there for 40 years. After paying her bills she was usually left with $3 to buy groceries.

Jane's first stop that morning was at the local bakery, Sugar Loaf. Mary was working behind the counter that day. She wanted a half loaf of fresh bread, but it was $4. That was $1 more than she had. As she thought about what to do, other customers arrived, and a line started to form. They heard what was happening, but no one stepped up to help her. These were all people that Jane knew since this was the type of town where everyone knew everyone else. Jane shyly looked up to Mary and asked how much cost if she bought 3 slices of bread. She told her that it would only be $3. Jane handed her the $3 from her pocket and left with 3 small slices of bread.

Jane lived on the other side of town in the small house that she and her husband, Jim, bought together 52 years prior. The house was in dire need of repair.

When she arrived home and was walking up the creaking boards leading up to the front porch, the board broke and she almost fell through.

She knew it was time to ask her neighbor, Fred, for assistance. He was a handyman and did small jobs for people in town. She had known Fred since his family moved to Leewood and he was still a high school student.

She told Fred what happened and asked how much it would cost to fix it. He barely looked up at her and responded $100.

"I don't have the much." Responded Jane.

"Then go get a job and then I'll fix it, along with anything else you need done," snapped Fred.

As so walked away, she mumbled to herself, *he was always a bully to everyone and hasn't changed a bit.*

She had to use the back door to get into her house. Once inside she slipped off her shoes and made a cup of tea. She reused the same tea bag repeatedly until there was nothing left to it. She squeezed every bit of tea from the bag. She added very little sugar. She tried to make it last as long as she could.

She took her mug of tea and went to relax in the living room. There were only a few pieces of furniture in the living room. One of them was Jim's rocker with faded blue cushions. Jane sat in the rocker across from his. Her heart ached as she thought about Jim. She missed him so much.

She sat back and thought about the past. They were so happy together. In high school, they were young and free. She reminisced about the day they met with friends, Judy and Danny, at the soda shop and talked about an upcoming school dance. She and Judy shared what their dresses looked like. Jim and Danny just talked about football. They were excited that school would be out soon. They made plans to go camping. At the campgrounds they selected there would be swimming, boating, and all types of games. Their friends, Jeff, Debbie, Molly, and Jason were joining them. Their friends across town, Matt, Laura, Jake, and Cindy, would meet them there. She remembered how she felt when they sat around the fire, singing songs, and sneaking kisses. It was always nice to look back on those days. Many of their friends left to get jobs in another state.

Jim and Jane stayed close. Their marriage was strong. Their mothers were friends in high school. In town, they had Sparkle, a small boutique, which was the go-to place to shop for dresses, shoes, and more. The girls were going to Penny's to get their hair and nails done. Penny's was the only beauty shop in town.

School dances were always held on Saturdays. The boys would pick them up and they all met at the school where the band, The 4 G's, were playing songs by Dion and the Belmonts, Fabian, and Bobby Rydell. It was an exciting night of music. Jim always looked so handsome in his black suit. Jane wore a pink short-sleeved dress. The dance ended at 11:00 and Jim promptly took Jane home. He gave her a gentle kiss goodnight that made her heart feel so good.

The next morning her family went to church. Pastor John delivered uplifting sermons every week. At the end of service, he stood by the door to shake everyone's hand as they left. When they arrived home, Jane changed out of her Sunday dress and slipped on comfy jeans before she left to meet her friends Debbie and Molly at the mall. Jane's mom gave her money for lunch and they spent 2 hours looking in stores and talking about what things would be like after they graduate.

When new people moved into town, the atmosphere seemed to change. The people in town once all had a bond. They looked out for each other. But not anymore. No one really did anything for anyone, unless they were getting paid.

The only things the town had going for it were Sugar Loaf, ShoeWorks, a thrift store called Patches, the GBA Gas Station/Garage, and the corner store, Heartwood Grocery. Jane knew that the town needed a lot of help. The people there were barely making it, financially. She prayed that one day things would change, that someone with money would come in and rescue the town.

She knew that she was mistreated by many because she was the poorest woman in town, but she forgave them. She felt their cold behavior even in church that Sunday. She did not have nice clothes like the others. At the end of church services, the congregation would gather in groups to talk to each other. But no one ever stopped to talk to her. So, she left quietly and embarked on the half-mile walk home, all alone.

The next day was Monday and she planned to go back to the bakery with her last few pennies and buy 2 slices of bread if Mary would sell them to her. After arriving from church, she made a cup of weak tea and sat in her recliner to read the Bible. As the hours passed, she washed her cup and decided to go to bed.

She woke early the next day, cleaned the living room then took a shower and got dressed. She left for her trip into town.

She stopped at Sugar Loaf to see if Mary would sell her a few slices of bread. Mary was talking to a tall man in a black suit.

Mary saw Jane walking in and said, "There she is right there."

Jane was confused as the man turned and asked, "Are you Jane Wilson?"

"Yes, but who are you?"

"My name is Joe Martin. I'm from New York. I work for attorney, Charles Johnson. I must speak with you. Can we go somewhere and talk?"

"Yes, we will go to my house. But I need to buy bread," she told him. She then looked over at Mary and asked, "Can I buy 2 slices of bread and a tea bag for two pennies, please?"

Joe looked at her concerned about her state. He interjected, "Mary, please give her a loaf of bread and a box of tea bags, I will pay for it," he continued, as he pulled out his wallet. He picked up the bag and asked Jane if she was ready to go, that his car was parked outside.

When they arrived at Jane's house, Fred was outside and gave a shocked look when he saw Jane getting out of the car. No one had ever come by to see her. He watched, speechless, as they walked to the back of the house. The front step was still broken.

When Joe walked inside, he noticed that there was only a little bit of furniture inside but it was extremely clean.

"Have a seat, "Jane directed. "Would like some tea and toast."

"That would be very nice, indeed," he responded.

She put the kettle of water on the stove. As she prepared the toast, she asked, "So, what is this all about?"

"I have some photos for you to look at."

She sat a plate of toast on the table and poured two cups of tea before she sat down.

He pulled photos and a laptop from his briefcase. He showed her the photos and asked of she knew them. There was a tall girl standing next to a dapper man in the photos. She did not recognize them and asked Joe who they were.

"Don't you know them," he questioned.

"No. Maybe you have the wrong Jane.

He pulled out another photo and handed it to her.

She was startled and said, "That's my cousin, Ruth."

"I knew I had the right Jane," he said.

"I only met her once. It was on Thanksgiving at our house. The whole family was together but fighting broke out and names started getting called, so dinner broke up early that day. I always wondered what happened to her. She was moving abroad to Paris after she got her degree. It was probably to get away from her family. I never heard more about her. I do hope that she is alright, that she got married and had children. She always seemed so sad.

Joe turned on his laptop and reached out to a gentleman in New York via Zoom. It was a man in his 50s in the video. He stated, "Mrs. Wilson, my name is Charles Johnson. I'm sorry to tell you that your cousin, Ruth, and her husband, Bob, died in a car accident a year ago. We were trying to find you, but we had very little information about you to go on. My man there wouldn't give up and he finally found you. We only had your maiden name, Grimes. Do you

9

know how many Grimes there are?" He chuckled at the thought. He went on to say, "But here we are, and I am so sorry for your loss. And I need you in my office tomorrow."

"Oh, I couldn't" responded Jane. "I am a poor widow and I have no money. I can't," she insisted as she shook her head.

"I understand," he said. "Joe, make sure she gets on the plane. Mrs. Wilson don't worry about the costs. I have it all covered. Just pack a bag and go with Joe. I will make all of the arrangements, including a hotel stay for you, and anything else you need."

Jane agreed and they ended the call. While Joe was calling the airport, Jane took a shower and put on the only nice suit she owned. It was a birthday gift from Jim. She only packed what she needed and handed her suitcase to Joe. He placed it in the trunk, and they were off.

Chapter 2

On the way to the airport, Jane asked what Mr. Johnson was like.

"He is 50 years old and has been married for 28 years. They have three great children. He is the kind of man who is always there to help people the best he can. I am blessed to be working for him. He treats me like I am family."

"Is that why he is helping me?"

"Sure is! When he heard about you and what happened, he insisted on helping you."

"How did he know about me? How did my cousin know him? It seems strange to me, with her living in another country and me here in America."

He looked at Jane and said, "That's not exactly true."

"What do you mean? I don't understand what's going on. I only met Ruth the one time that I told you about. When the arguing broke out, Ruth and I went to my room and had fun talking until her dad called out for her because they were going home."

At the airport, Jane continued to play over the day's events in her mind as they boarded the plane. She could not make sense of the things they said to her. She was nervous on the flight. This was her first time on a plane. She enjoyed the in-flight movie that was just ending when the plane landed in New York.

There was a car waiting for them at the airport. The driver, Nancy, smiled at Joe and shook Jane's hand stating, "It's so nice to meet you, Mrs. Wilson."

"Please, call me Jane."

"Okay, Jane, I am going to take you to your hotel. Joe will see that you get settled in. It's 11:00 now, I will pick you up at one. We'll go to lunch, do some sightseeing and then go out to dinner. Will that be alright?"

"That would be wonderful! Thank you!"

When they got to the hotel, Joe escorted her to her room which was 2 spacious rooms and a large bathroom.

Joe looked around the room and asked, "Is everything alright here for you?"

"Yes, you and Nancy have been so good to me."

"It's my pleasure, Jane. I will leave you to get some rest. Be sure to call room service for a pot of tea. And don't forget to ask for those little cakes, too. I will pick you up at 9:00 in the morning." As he walked to the door, he turned back around and said, "Enjoy your day."

Back home in Leewood, Fred pulled up to the Sugar Loaf and went inside to inquire about Jane. He was hoping someone knew who the man was that she was with and what he wanted her for. There were several people inside the bakery, and they all had questions about Jane.

"The man is from New York. He works for some big shot lawyer," Mary explained.

"Maybe someone left her some money," stated Pete, one of the men from town.

They all laughed at the notion.

"Who would leave her money," scoffed Fred. "No one is left from her family."

"Maybe it's someone on Jim's side," suggested Mary.

"I don't think so," said Fred. "All I know for sure is that she only gets a small pension from Jim's time at the factory.

"I hope someone left her some clothes. Anything would be better than what she has now," Mary joked.

Everyone laughed again.

Mary's friend, Clyde, jumped into the conversation. "Maybe Jim owed the IRS money for back taxes, and they want Jane to pay up or go to jail. Could you imagine seeing her on the 6:00 news? Her in handcuffs."

The room broke out in another burst of laughter.

The next day at the factory the employees learned that the factory may be relocating to another country due to slow sales and financial reasons. Chatter broke out in the room as they all started talking. They wondered what would happen to their homes, their children, and the small businesses they had on the side.

Clyde spoke up and said, "I can't afford to move. I'm still paying on my house."

"We still have some time. This won't happen for another year. Things may change" stated the foreman.

Chapter 3

The next day at Sugar Loaf, people gathered Sugar Loaf to talk about what was happening at ShoeWorks. They were up in arms and not sure about what to do.

Pastor John chimed in and said, "We need a miracle. We should call on the Lord for help. Anything can happen in a year."

They nodded in agreement and held hands as a group to pray. He led them in prayer "Father God, we come to you now and ask for your help for the town. This is all these people have. We ask for your blessings on the factory and the town. We only have one year for this to change. Nothing is impossible with you. There is nothing too small for you. We come now and ask all of this in Jesus name. Amen.

Back at the hotel, Jane was enjoying her pot of tea and cakes. She still wondered what this had to do with Ruth. *Poor thing to die like that. Both her and Bob, gone.*

Jane wished that they had more time together. We enjoyed the last conversation they had together. Ruth confided to her how her parents fought so much that she often thought of running away. She was so happy now that she was old enough to move away and Paris would be the perfect spot for her. She was moving the following week and would finally have peace and quiet. A few minutes later, her parents told her it was time to go home. They hugged each other goodbye. That was the last time she saw her. She was so glad that Ruth found a man who loved her and took care of her.

Just then the phone rang and broke the silence in the room. It was a worker from the front desk letting her know that Nancy was waiting for her. Jane told her to let Nancy know she would be right down, she got so busy in her own thoughts that she lost track of time. *Talk about being from the backwoods. I better keep my mind on what I am doing.*

She went down and thanked Nancy for taking her out.

"You're quite welcome, let's start by getting some lunch."

The first stop on their sightseeing tour was to see the Statue of Liberty. Jane was in awe at the beauty of the statue. It was amazing for her to see people from so many different ethnic backgrounds from all over the world.

As they drove away, Jane looked over and asked, "Are you ready to go shopping?"

Jane couldn't do it anymore, she had to tell her the truth. With tears in her eyes, she responded, "I don't have any money, none at all. I am so embarrassed."

Nancy pulled into a parking lot and gave Jane a big hug. "Don't worry, Mr. Johnson gave me a credit card to use.

Jane couldn't believe her ears. "Really?"

"Really. So, let's get going, and then we'll have dinner. They have a wonderful restaurant inside the mall."

Jane was in awe at how beautiful the mall looked inside. She wished they had something like this in Leewood. Everyone could move their small business inside the mall. She prayed a silent prayer. *Oh Lord, please help us. We need something more than the shoe factory. I know that you answer prayers. I know they have been unkind to me, but I forgive them Just like you told us to do. I ask this in Jesus name. Amen.*

Jane looked at the line of stores in the mall and said, "This is so big."

"It sure is," she laughed. She took Jane by the arm, and they proceeded down the hall.

There were three floors of shops filled with stores. They stopped at five shops until they picked the one to start at.

"Look, Jane, they have a little bit of everything inside. There were clothes, shoes, purses, and jewelry. So much to look at!"

The sales lady approached them. "Good morning, ladies. My name is Sally, can I help you find anything?"

Nancy responded, "Yes, we need at least 10 outfits for Jane, preferably pantsuits. And let Jane pick out six dresses. And we want shoes to match each dress. Oh, and matching jewelry, including rings, bracelets, and necklaces. She will also need 2 large suitcases."

Sally explained that she would have everything waiting for them in the front while we shopped. They shopped for three hours. When they were finished, they took the many packages and suitcases to the car. They were just able to squeeze everything into the trunk and then went back inside for dinner. It was a wonderful day for Jane.

As they sat down to eat, Jane asked, "Why is Mr. Johnson doing all of this?

"I guess he has his reasons," shrugged Jane. "He will explain everything in the morning."

They enjoyed their meal as they reminisced about the day.

They drove back to the hotel and Nancy went inside to get someone to help her carry the packages.

Two porters came out with a cart and took Jane's bags to her room.

In the room, Jane let out a happy sigh, "Thank you so much, Nancy, for all you did for me today."

"I really did enjoy it. Well, I'll let you get some rest. I'll see you in the morning. Good night!"

Jane looked around the room at all of the boxes and was in shock. It was all so surreal. It took her three hours to go through everything. She put together the suit she wanted to wear the next day. It was a pink and white top with white pants and pink shoes. She had a pink purse to match her outfit. She selected a pearl necklace to wear with it. She had matching earrings, a necklace, and a ring. Everything looked so pretty together. Jane had not had anything new in years. She was overwhelmed with gratitude that people would do all of this for her, and strangers at that.

She wondered why all of this was happening to her. What were Ruth and Bob into that involved her? She hoped that she could get some sleep. She had a big day tomorrow.

Chapter 4

Jane slept well. At 5:00, the phone rang, waking her up from her sleep. It was her 5:00 wake-up call. She woke up feeling great! She took a shower and called room service to order more tea and little cakes for breakfast. It arrived in five minutes.

The server came in and introduced himself as Robbie. He set up a table for her and cleared the dishes from the night before.

"Did you have a good night's rest?" He asked.

"I did, thank you so much for everything," Jane responded.

Before he turned to leave, he smiled and said, "Have a blessed day."

"You too, Robbie," smiled Jane.

As she sat down to enjoy her cakes, she realized this was a fresh pot of tea. I didn't have to reuse a tea bag to get this. First, she prayed to God. *Thank you, Lord, for this day. I don't know what this day will bring but I know you will be in it. Thank You. Amen*

By 7:00, she had finished her breakfast and went to finish getting dressed. She was so happy with how well the clothes fit her. It was like they were made for her.

At 9:00 the phone rang again. It was Sue from the front desk letting her know that a gentleman was there to pick her up.

"Please let him know I will be right down," said Jane.

When she got to the lobby, she saw Joe waiting for her.

"Miss Jane, look at you. I hardly recognized you. What a change. That color pink is just your color." He stated.

"Thank you, very much! I couldn't believe it was me either."

They both laughed. Jane looked over to Sue and thanked her.

Joe held the door open for her as they walked to the car. Jane asked if he could tell her about anything that was going to happen that day, but he could not.

As they pulled in front of a tall building, Joe stated, "We are here Miss Jane."

He got out of the car and opened the door for her.

Jane looked up at the tall steel and glass building that was 24 stories high, and said, "We don't have buildings this big in Leewood."

"For us outsiders, everything looks big in small towns." He looked at Jane and asked, "Are you ready? This is your big day to find out what this day is all about.

As they walked in, Jane looked around the lobby at the brown leather couches lined up across from a row of large leather chairs. There were several glass tables in between them. There were brass lamps on the small tables that separated the chairs.

He led her into one of the offices where Nancy was sitting at a large oak desk. She jumped up to give Jane a hug and a kiss on the cheek.

"You look lovely. Come, he's waiting for us." She stated as she walked Jane over to another door that led to an even larger office.

Mr. Johnson rose from the desk and held out his hand to shake hands with Jane. "Miss Jane, I have waited a long time to meet you, please have a seat."

"Thank you, Mr. Johnson, I have been anxious to ask you, what is this all about and what does my cousin Ruth have to do with this?"

"Miss Jane, when was the last time you saw Ruth?"

"I met her once on Thanksgiving at my parent's house. She was standing by herself, so I went up to introduce myself. She said she was my cousin, from my father's side. She said that our fathers are brothers. I asked if she went to school here, and she said that she went to school in Paris. She was about to graduate but was planning to stay in Paris to work. Everything was going great and then a fight broke out between our families. They left soon after and I never saw her again. Mr. Johnson...."

"Please call me, Chuck, everyone does," he said. "I know you are excited to find out what is going on, let me start by telling you that Ruth did stay in Paris. There she met Bob Morris, who would become her husband. I knew Bob personally; we went to school together. Bob came from a rich family. They had stock in oil and a portfolio in several large industries. After Bob and Ruth were married, they moved back to his estate in Texas. When Bob's parents died, he took over the company's business handlings. Everything was left to Bob and his brother, Paul, but Paul has dementia and has been in a nursing home. Bob has made sure that he is well taken care of.

"That must have been hard for Bob to see his brother like that."

"It was. Bob and Ruth were close to Paul. They were a tight-knit family. Bob and Ruth often helped others in need, as well. They had such kind hearts. They helped all over the world, wherever there was a need. That is a little bit about their background."

20

"That's wonderful. It's so sad that they died. Tell me more about the accident that killed them."

"It was late at night and raining out. Bob was going around a curve and lost control of his car. He went over an embankment and hit a tree. They were killed instantly. Witnesses called 911 and stayed at the site until the police arrived. At the morgue, they found my business card in Bob's pocket and asked me to come down to identify their bodies. That was a year ago. I am so sorry for your loss. Bob and Ruth were good friends of mine and I miss them very much."

"Oh, what a shame, those poor things. I'm glad she met someone and had a good life. It sounds like she was so happy."

"Oh, believe me, Jane, they were meant for each other."

"But, Chuck, you said this happened a year ago."

"Yes, we have been looking for you for a year."

"Chuck were there any children."

"No, they didn't have any children. Not that they didn't try. It just didn't happen for them. I have their will that I need to read to you. They want their home and everything inside to be sold and donated to a charity that they selected. I will take care of all of those arrangements. Ruth told Bob that it was important to her that they leave you something. Their will states that you are to receive all their stocks and bonds and all of their money in the bank."

"Oh, Chuck! How nice of them to think of me."

"Yes, it was nice of them. She was worried that you and your husband might be low on funds."

"Oh, she was right about that."

"We set up a trust fund for you at our bank, here in the city, and whenever you need money, no matter how much it is, we will have it transferred to your bank in Leewood."

"Chuck, will there be enough for me to buy a car?"

"Jane, there will be enough money for you to buy as many cars as you want."

"What do you mean?"

"Nancy, stand beside her, you too, Joe." He directed. "Jane, they left you 1.2 billion dollars."

Jane gasped and her mouth dropped open, yet she was speechless."

"Miss Jane, are you alright? Do you need a drink of water?"

"No, I need a drink of Jack Daniels. Are you telling me I'm a billionaire? I can't believe it!"

"Miss Jane, if you like I can have one million dollars transferred to your bank right now."

"No, please, I don't want my bank to know anything. It will be all over town before I get home."

"When you get home, select a car lot that you want to purchase your car from and have them call me."

"I still can't believe this."

"Just think Miss Jane, no more weak tea or three slices of bread." Stated Joe.

"Oh, Joe, no more broken steps. No more asking for handouts. No more people treating me bad anymore. But this is all a work of God. Now I can save my town and build it the way it should be. Oh, what a blessing. But it's so sad about Bob and Ruth dying like that."

"I agree Jane." He presented Jane with paperwork to sign and copies for her to take home.

"Well, I'm ready to go home, and see what is going on, and to let all of this sink in. What a morning!"

I understand Miss Jane, and it was nice to meet you. By the way, I have something for you." He handed her an envelope that contained $1,000. "Just in case you need something now. Joe will arrange for your flight home. And remember to call me anytime you need money. We are here to help you."

"Thank you. All of you, for your kindness.

Nancy drove Jane back to the hotel and walked her to her room.

"Get some rest, Miss Jane, I will pick you up when Joe has your ticket and flight number together. So, I will see you later."

"I'll be ready," stated Jane. She then walked inside the room and sat down to take in everything that just happened. *So much money. I can't even picture what that would be. What would the people back home say about me now?"*

Jane called room service and ordered a pot of tea and a club sandwich. She needed something to calm her down.

She was happy to see that Robbie was her server again. He came in and set the table for her.

"Robbie, I will be leaving this afternoon. Thank you for everything."

"You take care. Have a blessed and safe flight home.

Jane wanted to have everything ready when Nancy came to pick her up.

As she sipped her tea, she wondered what she should do first when she got home. What will Fred say when he sees her new car? What will Mary say when she buys a whole loaf of bread instead of a few slices? What will her neighbors think when she sees her new clothes? There won't be any more hand-me-downs for her. Wait until they see that she is not the same person she was when she left. She could now buy the nice house by the park where the shopping center used to be.

God, thank you so much for your blessings. I could never do this without you. You are always there when I need you. Thank you.

As she soaked in the events of the day, the phone rang. It was Nancy letting her know that she was on the way. She asked Jane to meet her in the lobby. When they hung up, Jane called the front desk and asked Sue if someone could take her luggage to the lobby for her.

Five minutes later, two porters were there to carry her luggage and escort Jane to the lobby.

As Jane waited in a chair for Nancy, Sue approached her.

"I hope you enjoyed your stay," said Sue. "How was your everything?"

"Everything was wonderful Everyone was so kind to me. Thank you."

When Nancy arrived, Jane said goodbye to the hotel staff. They placed the suitcases in Nancy's car and left for the airport.

On their way to the airport, Nancy informed Jane that her flight leaves at 3:00 and since it was only 1:30, they would have time to talk at the airport before she had to board her flight.

Once at the airport, they chatted as they watched planes come and go.

"What will you do now when you get home," asked Nancy.

"I think I will buy a car. I usually have to call someone for a ride, or I walk. Not anymore. It still doesn't feel real.

"Well, take it one day at a time. Joe arranged for a cab to pick you up at the airport. It's already paid for."

When they heard the call for Jane's flight the ladies hugged each other goodbye.

"Thank you, Nancy, for everything."

"You're welcome, have a blessed flight."

Chapter 5

Sure enough, there was a cab waiting for Jane at the airport. She directed the driver to take her to the nearest car lot.

She wheeled her suitcases inside and approached the salesman by the door. He introduced himself as Jack.

"I am interested in the red car right there." She pointed to a candy apple red
Toyota Camry. "How much is it?"

Jack smiled and said, "That car is $32,000."

"Great! I will take it," said Jane. She handed him a business card and said, "You need to call Mr. Johnson. He handles my financial affairs and will have the money transferred to you."

He took the card from Jane and escorted her to a seat at his desk while he made the call. "I'll draw up the paperwork and you can take your car home. It won't take long at all."

It took about a half hour to complete the sale. Jack escorted her to her new Camry and helped put her suitcases in the back.

As she drove away, she smiled as she again realized there was no more walking for her. *Wait until they see me at church tomorrow.*

She pulled into the driveway of her home and carried the suitcases inside. Everything was exactly as she left it. She left her suitcases unpacked and decided to go shopping.

She wished her town had a mall so she would not have to drive so far. But she sure was happy to have a car again.

She spent several hours shopping before returning home. She put everything away from her shopping spree and unpacked her suitcases. Afterward, she took a shower and made a pot of tea. She wanted to go to bed early. She was exhausted. Before going to bed, she thanked the Lord for the good people she met and for the wonderful day.

The next morning, she woke up early, got dressed, and made another cup of tea before leaving for church.

When she arrived at church, the parking lot was full. She wondered what was happening. Did she miss something? When she entered everyone was shouting. So, she took a seat next to her friend, Becky, and asked what was going on.

"They are going to close the factory." Becky explained.

"What? That makes no sense," stated Jane.

"If they do, I don't know what we'll do. We might have to sell our house because there is nothing else here."

"No one is going to come here and save the factory. Where will we go? What will we do?"

Jane could not believe what was happening. She heard Fred yelling at someone in the front of the church but through the crowd, she could not see who it was. Becky informed her that it was the foreman at ShoeWorks.

"Maybe I can talk to him and see what can be done," said Jane.

"What can you do? You don't have two pennies to rub together." She looked up and down at Jane's clothes and said, "They must have gotten new clothes in at the store. Did that cost you your last penny?"

Jane laughed as she said a silent prayer. *Lord, help me. I need your strength right now. I can help these people and save this town. Thank you for providing the money. I give you all the glory.*

She tried to speak up, but no one could hear her. So, she spoke a little louder and soon the room got quiet while they were all looking at her.

"I would like to speak to the foreman, if I may," Jane announced.

Everyone started to laugh and make snarky comments.

Fred spoke up, saying, "The poor widow wants to talk. Why don't you just go home? You don't have any say here. Everyone knows that you don't have anything. We just tolerate you."

"Do you speak for everyone?" asked Jane. She looked around the room asking, "Does Fred speak for all of you? Speak up. Now is your chance to tell me to my face."

They all just looked down.

"That's what I thought," Fred responded.

"Shut up, Fred, and sit down," shouted Jane angrily.

She then turned to approach the foreman, a 60-year-old man who was short in stature and had salt-and-pepper hair.

"Hi, my name is Jane Wilson."

"Larry. It's nice to meet you."

"Could we meet in your office in the morning?"

Fred interrupted, "You can't do that. We have to know what this is all about first. And why does this concern you? You're nothing."

This time Larry interjected. "That's enough. I'm tired of hearing your mouth. One more word out of you and you're fired. Do I make myself clear? Well, do I?"

"Yes sir," Fred grunted.

"Good. And, Jane, I will see you in the morning. Good day." And with that, he left.

No one said a word as the Pastor called everyone to come together for the sermon.

When she got home, she did not see hide or hair of Fred. She rearranged a few things to make room for the items she bought the day before. When she finished, she started dinner.

She mulled over what happened at church. She did not realize that things had gotten so bad in the few days that she was gone. *Lord, show me how to help these people, even if they don't deserve it. I forgive all of them. Amen.*

Chapter 6

Jane woke up early the next day. After she got washed and dressed, she left for the bakery.

She pulled into Sugar Loaf, parked her car, and went inside. There were several men from town there.

"Mary, I will have a large tea and 2 mini cakes to go. I will sit at that table in the corner waiting."

Buck, one of the men asked what she was planning on doing at the board meeting.

"I don't know, yet."

Buck responded, "Miss Jane, you better think of something before you get there or they will laugh you out the door."

They all laughed, even Mary, who was just bringing Jane her tea and cakes.

"See that car out there," said Jane, "that's mine, all paid for. See these clothes? They're not hand-me-downs, not anymore. I'm not the same person I was when I left here. A new Jane has come back to town. I'm not the same Jane who bought three slices of bread for $3 or drank tea using the same tea bag until there was nothing left. All you and Mary did was laugh and make jokes when you thought I wasn't listening. It hurt, but I wouldn't let you see how much. Well, I have to go to my meeting. But I'll tell you this. I forgave all of you. Mary, here is $20 for the tea and cakes, keep the change."

She left the bakery, got in her car, and drove away.

When she got to the factory, Larry was waiting for her.

"Good morning, Mrs. Wilson. How are you?"

"I'm fine, thank you. Is everyone here?"

"Yes, we are. Are you ready?

"Yes, I am."

"Great! Have a seat. Gentleman, this is Mrs. Wilson."

"Just call me Jane."

The gentleman in the first seat spoke up. "Well, Jane, I'm Michael but everyone calls me Big Mike from when I played football for the Rams. I own this factory. I used to come here as a boy to help my father. We had a lot of good times. He passed a few years back."

"I'm so sorry to hear that. My husband, Jim, worked here for 17 years." She spoke.

Mike smiled, "Yes, Jim Wilson. I remember him. He was a good worker. I talked to him often. He was a good man. I'm sorry for your loss."

"What can we do for you?" Larry interjected. "You said you wanted to talk to us."

"Yes, I do. Mike, what would it take to keep the factory here?"

"Well, as you can see, there is nothing really here. There are no stores or malls to draw people here, even though we are right near the highway. It would take a miracle to build this place up and millions of dollars to keep us here."

"Mike, how much," Jane asked again.

"Jane, too much, and we couldn't raise it."

"Mike, I asked you how much."

"Jane, what can you do? Nothing. We can't have a fundraiser in this town."

"Mike, how much?"

"Okay, Jane, 50 million."

"I'm glad you stopped beating around the bush. Now give me that phone."

She put in a call to Chuck's office.

"Hi Nancy, is Chuck in?"

31

"Yes, he is. I'll put you right through Miss Jane."

"Hi. Miss Jane. How are you? What can I do for you?"

Jane filled him in on what was happening and the 50 million dollars she needed to save the factory.

"Put Mike on the phone."

She handed the phone to Mike.

"This is Mike." "You're a lawyer," he asked into the phone. "I told Jane what we need. It's a lot of money. We can't raise that much. That's what I told her, 50 million. Why yes, in Charleston. You're kidding?! Is this for real?" A big grin came across Mike's face. "Here she is," he stated as he handed the phone to Jane "He wants to talk to you."

"Hello," Jane said into the phone.

"Everything is taken care of. Is there anything else I can do for you?" asked Chuck.

"No, Chuck, this is good. Thank you! Goodbye."

Mike then announced, "Gentlemen, we are not moving the factory and we have a new member. Jane Wilson now holds the largest share of stock in ShoeWorks. Jane, I would like you to meet Tom Smith, Chris Burns, Don Green, and Harry Meyers."

Each of the men stood up to shake her hand.

"Pleased to meet all of you," declared Jane. "Now, if you'll excuse me, I have a lot more to do today. Thank you for meeting with me and have a blessed day."

"Good day, Jane," said Mike as he stood up to shake her hand. "Thank you very much for what you did for our plant and all the workers. You have a blessed day, too."

As Jane walked back to her car, she said another silent prayer. *Well, Lord, thank you for the money to help the people of Leewood. And I want to thank Ruth and her husband. I'm just sorry I didn't get to see her again before she died.*

There was one more stop she needed to make. That was to see George. He owned the house that she wanted to buy.

She drove by the house she adored. She saw that it needed some work done on it but she could fix whatever needed to be done. She continued on to George's house.

She found George sitting on the porch. When she got out of the car he was surprised at her new look.

"Miss Jane, is that you? What happened to you? You sure have changed. Get up here and let me get a look at you."

She smiled as she walked up the steps. "Oh, George" she stated.

"Wow, you look nice. Did you hit the lottery or something?"

"Well, something," she stated.

"Tell me about it. Here, have a seat in the rocker while I get you some lemonade."

"Thank you," she said.

"I'll be right back, make yourself at home."

A few minutes later, he came back out with two tall glasses of cold lemonade and handed one to Jane.

"So, Miss Jane, what brings you here?"

"Well, George, I want to talk to you about the house you have for sale on the corner lot of Springhouse Drive. I want to buy it."

"But Jane it needs work. It should be torn down and rebuilt."

"George, it's a nice house. It just needs some help."

"Jane, what else is on your mind? There's something else besides the house. Out with it. What is it?"

"Alright. Let's take a walk."

"Sure," said George. He put his arm around hers and led her down the steps.

As they walked, she pointed to the open field across from his home. It was wide open land that George owned.

"I want this property. Can you imagine a mall being here? A McDonald's. A Wendy's. Gas Stations. Restaurants. And people from all over coming here to shop."

"But Miss Jane, you would have to dig up every inch of this land. Do you know how much that would cost? Not to mention all the costs of the house."

"I know having a mall here has been your dream since high school."

"This location is right next to the state highway. Cars pass here all the time. A mall would help our town and put the people to work."

"Yes, it has always been my dream. Please help me to make my dream come true."

"Jane, it would cost a lot of money that you don't have."

"George, just give me a price for both."

"Well, it's a lot but it can happen for 1.5 million."

"So, there it is. Let's go back to your house and make a phone call." She smiled brightly.

Two Years Later

Jane and George sat on Jane's new porch, enjoying cold glasses of lemonade. They watched the bustling activity at the new mall across the street. Shoppers hurried in and out of stores, kids excitedly pointed at the colorful displays, and the scent of fresh pretzels wafted through the air. As the sun set, the mall's lights flickered on, casting a warm glow on the scene and creating a lively, inviting atmosphere. Jane and George chatted about their plans for the weekend, feeling content and relaxed.

Made in the USA
Middletown, DE
26 August 2024